FlashRevise
Pocketbook

GCSE Business Studies

Philip Allan Updates, an imprint of Hodder Education, an Hachette UK company, Market Place, Deddington, Oxfordshire OX15 0SE

Orders

Bookpoint Ltd, 130 Milton Park, Abingdon, Oxfordshire OX14 4SB
tel: 01235 827720   fax: 01235 400454   e-mail: uk.orders@bookpoint.co.uk

Lines are open 9.00 a.m.–5.00 p.m., Monday to Saturday, with a 24-hour message answering service. You can also order through our website: www.philipallan.co.uk

© Philip Allan Updates 2009
ISBN 978-1-4441-0183-6

First published in 2004 as *Flashrevise Cards*

Impression number 5 4 3 2 1
Year   2014   2013   2012   2011   2010   2009

Printed in Spain

Hachette UK's policy is to use papers that are natural, renewable and recyclable products and made from wood grown in sustainable forests. The logging and manufacturing processes are expected to conform to the environmental regulations of the country of origin.

P01594

Starting Up

1 Enterprise
2 Entrepreneur
3 Start-up risks
4 Business plan
5 Start-up market research
6 Start-up business objectives
7 Start-up location
8 Start-up finance
9 Adding value
10 Opportunity cost
11 Competition
12 Primary sector
13 Secondary sector
14 Tertiary sector
15 Government intervention

Forms of Business

16 Functions of business
17 Legal forms of business
18 Sole trader
19 Partnership
20 Company
21 Shareholder
22 Director
23 Private limited company
24 Public limited company
25 Limited liability
26 Franchise

Objectives

27 Aims and objectives
28 Stakeholders
29 Stakeholder friendly business
30 Business ethics
31 Unethical behaviour
32 External costs
33 SWOT analysis
34 Business growth
35 Takeover

Marketing

36 Marketing
37 Demand
38 Market research
39 Market share
40 Market segments
41 Product life cycle
42 Extension strategies
43 Product portfolio
44 Marketing mix
45 Penetration pricing
46 Promotion
47 Promotional activities
48 Distribution channel
49 New product development
50 e-commerce

Finance

51 Sources of finance
52 Loan
53 Net cash flow
54 Cash-flow forecasting
55 Profit and loss account
56 Revenue
57 Costs
58 Loss
59 Profitability
60 Gross profit
61 Breakeven
62 Balance sheet
63 Current assets
64 Liquidity

People

65 Organisational chart
66 Span of control
67 Levels of hierarchy
68 Centralisation
69 Management style
70 Delegation
71 Communication
72 Recruitment
73 Selection
74 Remuneration
75 Non-monetary benefits
76 Training

77 Induction training
78 Trade union
79 Motivation
80 Maslow

Production

81 Production
82 Location
83 Capacity
84 Economies of scale
85 Diseconomies of scale
86 Stocks
87 Stock control
88 Division of labour
89 Quality
90 Lean production
91 ICT

External Environment

92 External environment
93 Interest rates
94 Taxes
95 European Union (EU)
96 Exchange rates
97 Legislation
98 Health and Safety at Work Act
99 Consumer protection legislation
100 Environmental responsibilities of business

Enterprise

Q1 State two possible sources of ideas for a new business.

Q2 State two reasons why a government might encourage start-up enterprises.

Q3 State two reasons, apart from profit, why someone may start up a business.

Q4 State two reasons why many start-up businesses fail.

ability to see a business opportunity and willingness to take a risk to pursue it

A1 inspiration; hobbies; seeing this type of business somewhere else; having a problem that is not solved by existing businesses

A2 creates jobs; creates competition for existing firms; reduces the number of people claiming unemployment benefit; helps to create new products and growth in the economy

A3 enjoyment; creating something for society; sense of achievement; being your own boss

A4 poor understanding of the market; competitors' actions; poor planning; lack of appropriate skills; changes in the economy

***examiner's* note** Some people are better than others at seeing business opportunities, but even they may not be willing to take the risk of developing a new business idea.

1 ANSWERS

Entrepreneur

Q1 State reasons why people set up their own business.

Q2 State two qualities that are needed to be an entrepreneur.

Q3 State two difficulties of setting up in business on your own.

Q4 State two sources of finance when setting up a new business.

ANSWERS

someone who takes risks and sets up a new business venture

A1 to be their own boss; to achieve something; to gain more rewards

A2
- determination
- willingness to take risks
- initiative
- ability to plan

A3
- raising finance
- lack of experience
- stress

A4
- friends
- family
- savings
- borrowing

***examiner's* note** Entrepreneurs are valuable to an economy as they create new products for customers, they create competition in markets and they create jobs.

(2) **ANSWERS**

Start-up risks

Q1 State two sources of ideas for a new business.

Q2 What is meant by a market niche?

Q3 State two reasons why new businesses often fail.

Q4 State two ways in which the government could encourage start-ups.

ANSWERS

the dangers of setting up a new business such as losing your investment

A1
- your experience
- your creativity
- other firms
- consumers

A2 a small segment of a market (small group of similar needs)

A3
- lack of experience
- competitors' actions
- lack of planning
- lack of finance
- limited market research

A4
- provide advice
- lend money
- offer tax cuts or subsidies
- provide access to cheap finance

***examiner's* note** To reduce the risk of starting up, entrepreneurs should undertake market research (either desk and/or field).

(3) **ANSWERS**

Business plan

Q1 State two elements of a business plan.

Q2 State two benefits of having a business plan.

Q3 State two reasons why a business plan may prove inaccurate.

Q4 Who might be interested in seeing a business plan?

ANSWERS

a document that sets out what a business wants to achieve and how to do it

A1
- financial analysis (e.g. cash-flow forecast)
- market analysis
- strategy
- objectives

A2
- helps organise activities
- helps anticipate problems
- can show to potential investors
- can review progress

A3
- changes in the market
- unforeseen problems (e.g. with quality)
- competitors' actions
- may be badly produced due to lack of experience

A4 employees, banks and investors; managers should also review it regularly

examiner's note A business plan needs to be regularly reviewed and updated throughout the life of the business as conditions change and new objectives and strategies are needed.

 ANSWERS

Start-up market research

Q1 Why is start-up market research often undertaken on a small scale?

Q2 What is desk research?

Q3 State one advantage of desk research compared to field research.

Q4 State two ways in which a small business might undertake market research.

ANSWERS

occurs when start-up businesses gather data about the market and their potential customers

A1 lack of finance and time

A2 secondary research, i.e. uses data already collected

A3 can be cheaper; can be quicker

A4 • telephone and other surveys
   • customer/supplier feedback
   • internet research
   • questionnaires
   • focus groups

***examiner's* note** Market research is often very important to make sure a market exists and to develop a focused marketing mix. It should reduce the risk of mistakes being made.

5 ANSWERS

Start-up business objectives

Q1 How is profit measured?

Q2 State two possible start-up business objectives apart from profit.

Q3 State two reasons for setting objectives.

Q4 What is a written business plan?

A1 profit = revenue − costs

A2
- survival
- breakeven
- maintain sufficient cash
- build the brand/reputation

A3
- to provide a target
- to review progress
- to help plan
- to help coordinate actions

A4 a document that sets out what a business aims to achieve and how it intends to do this; it includes an analysis of the market and the firm's strengths

***examiner's* note** Setting targets and producing a business plan do not guarantee business success (nothing can), but they help entrepreneurs to anticipate problems and prepare for and respond to them more effectively, which reduces the risk of failure.

Start-up location

Q1 State two reasons why finding a good location can be difficult when starting up.

Q2 State two factors that might affect the choice of a start-up location.

Q3 State one type of business that will want to locate near its customers. Why?

Q4 How does the internet affect location? Why?

ANSWERS

A1
- lack of finance
- established businesses may have the best locations already

A2 costs; customers' location; suppliers' location; infrastructure; impact on sales; the availability of raw materials; transport; labour; competition/other businesses; technology

A3 retailers (e.g. cafés, clothes shops, shoe shops); customers will not travel very far to buy products from these stores

A4 can reach people all over the world via the internet; customers do not have to visit physically, so there is more choice of location

***examiner's* note** The location of a start-up business may affect its costs (e.g. because of rent) and demand (e.g. depends if it is accessible to customers); this can affect its success. A hotel or café in the wrong place will struggle to survive.

7 **ANSWERS**

Start-up finance

Q1 State two ways in which a start-up business might raise finance.

Q2 State two problems a start-up business might have raising finance.

Q3 Why might a start-up business have cash-flow problems?

Q4 State two factors that might influence which source of finance to choose.

ANSWERS

money required to get a business established

A1 • overdraft
  • bank loans and mortgages
  • grants
  • loans from friends and family

A2 • lack of experience and track record so people are not willing to lend
  • may lack collateral (security)
  • may be perceived as high risk

A3 have to spend to develop the idea and launch it; early sales may be relatively low, so cash-flow problems

A4 • availability of money from different sources
  • cost, terms and conditions
  • whether owners lose any control (e.g. by bringing in outside investors)

***examiner's* note** Managing finances can be particularly difficult when setting up a business. It is difficult to raise money, suppliers insist on being paid quickly and customers may insist on being given time to pay.

 ANSWERS

Adding value

Q1 What is a market?

Q2 Identify the factors of production.

Q3 Distinguish between a 'good' and a 'service'.

Q4 State three factors that might influence the location of a hotel.

ANSWERS

the process of adding worth to a product that a customer is willing to pay for

A1 when buyers and sellers come together to trade

A2 land, labour, enterprise and capital

A3 a good is a physical product; a service is intangible and cannot physically be touched

A4 • land prices
- ease of access by road, rail and plane
- number of visitors to the area
- location relative to tourist attractions
- type of hotel (e.g. business, family)

***examiner's* note** There are a wide range of businesses: large/small, sole trader/company, manufacturer/service. Firms also behave in many different ways because they operate in such different markets.

9 ANSWERS

Opportunity cost

Q1 Why does holding cash have an opportunity cost?

Q2 A company can either keep its profits or pay them to shareholders as a d....................

Q3 If a firm invests in new equipment, what might be the opportunity cost?

Q4 If you carry on to study A-levels, what is the opportunity cost?

ANSWERS

A1 because the money could be earning interest in a bank

A2 dividend

A3 could have invested in advertising or developed new products

A4 the money you could have earned in a job whilst you are studying

***examiner's* note** When investing in a project, a firm might consider the opportunity cost of leaving the money in the bank – the interest rate. This means that when the interest rate increases, the opportunity cost does too – there is more incentive to save money and less incentive to use it elsewhere.

Competition

Q1 State three benefits for customers of greater competition.

Q2 State one disadvantage for firms of greater competition in their market.

Q3 State three actions that a firm might take if it is losing sales.

Q4 How can a firm increase its competitiveness?

ANSWERS

the extent to which rival firms compete for customers

A1 • more innovation
• lower prices
• better customer service

A2 lower sales; less profits; more difficult to get customers

A3 • cut price
• promote more
• look for new ways of distributing the product
• improve the product

A4 offer better value for money; provide better-quality goods or service; offer a unique product; innovate

examiner's note The amount of competition in a market depends on how easy it is for firms to set up in business (e.g. costs and whether any special skills or licences are needed).

(11) ANSWERS

Primary sector

Q1 Which of the following is a primary sector business: a farm, school, or a car manufacturer?

Q2 Name two other sectors in an economy apart from primary.

Q3 Is the primary sector in the UK relatively large or small?

Q4 A firm makes a loss if the c............... are greater than the r..............

ANSWERS

A1 farm

A2 • secondary
• tertiary

A3 small

A4 costs; revenue

examiner's note The primary sector is often quite big in less developed economies that rely on agriculture or minerals for their income. In the UK, the largest part of the economy is the tertiary sector, i.e. services such as education, banking and tourism.

Secondary sector

Q1 Who works in the secondary sector: a worker in a factory or a waiter in a restaurant?

Q2 The service sector of the economy is called the t............ sector.

Q3 Secondary businesses produce physical g............ rather than services.

Q4 If the revenue from sales is greater than the c............, the firm has made a p............

ANSWERS

A1 worker in a factory

A2 tertiary

A3 goods

A4 costs; profit

***examiner's* note** Manufacturing is likely to involve relatively high levels of investment in machinery (i.e. it is capital intensive). Managing a manufacturing process involves decisions such as what equipment to buy, what volume to produce, and how many stocks to hold. Customers nowadays demand more variety, which requires more flexible production.

(13) ANSWERS

Tertiary sector

Q1 Who works in the tertiary sector: a miner or an accountant?

Q2 Is the tertiary sector the largest or smallest sector in the UK?

Q3 Tertiary businesses produce s............... rather than goods.

Q4 The factors of production are l..........., l..........., c............... and
e.......................

ANSWERS

A1 accountant

A2 largest

A3 services

A4 land, labour, capital and enterprise

***examiner's* note** The tertiary sector usually involves a high level of direct contact with customers and a large labour input (i.e. it is labour intensive). The secondary sector by comparison involves more machinery and stocks. One problem of the service sector is dealing with different numbers of customers at different times of the day, the week and the year. Problems anticipating the level of demand is one reason why queues occur.

Government intervention

Q1 State two ways in which the government intervenes in an economy.

Q2 State two reasons why the government might encourage entrepreneurs.

Q3 State two ways in which the government might encourage entrepreneurs.

Q4 State two problems that individuals might have in setting up a business.

ANSWERS

occurs when the government affects business activity and behaviour

A1 • by introducing laws
• taxes or subsidies
• by directly providing products

A2 because they create jobs; pay tax; provide new goods and services; create competition

A3 • providing information and advice
• providing grants and subsidies

A4 • difficult getting finance
• lack experience
• face the competition of bigger firms

examiner's **note** Products that governments often provide include health, education, the police and the armed forces. Government organisations often have social objectives rather than focusing on profits.

 ANSWERS

Functions of business

Q1 State two ways in which marketing can affect the production process.

Q2 State two ways in which marketing decisions can affect the finances of a firm.

Q3 State two ways in which the way people are managed can affect the success of a firm.

Q4 State four ways of measuring the success of a business.

ANSWERS

A1 • may influence what is produced
  • may affect quantity produced
  • may affect the quality requested
  • may affect how much can be spent producing a product

A2 • may influence the revenue of the firm (e.g. by affecting how many units are sold)
  • influences costs (e.g. spending on marketing campaigns)

A3 • can affect productivity
  • can affect the quality of work and customer service

A4 • profits • turnover • growth • customer satisfaction
  • environmental impact

examiner's note The different functions of a business are interrelated. If marketing is successful, for example, it may mean more staff are required (human resources) and the firm has to increase capacity (production).

(16) ANSWERS

Legal forms of business

Q1 State two factors an entrepreneur might consider when deciding whether to be a sole trader or set up a company.

Q2 Who owns a company?

Q3 What is a Deed of Partnership?

Q4 What is unlimited liability?

ANSWERS

A1 • the need for outside investors
• the need for limited liability
• the desire to keep accounts private

A2 shareholders

A3 sets out the rights of the partners (e.g. the division of profits and what happens if a partner wants to leave the business)

A4 there is no limit to the liability of the owners; they could lose all their possessions if the business failed

***examiner's* note** Entrepreneurs have to decide on the best legal form of business for them. This depends on whether they want to share control, whether they need outside finance, how much risk is involved, whether they need the status of a company and whether they want and can afford to produce accounts.

 **17** **ANSWERS**

Sole trader

Q1 State two benefits of being a sole trader.

Q2 State two disadvantages of being a sole trader.

Q3 Give three problems of starting up a business.

Q4 Why do people set up their own businesses?

ANSWERS

A1 • fast decision making
• keep all the rewards

A2 • unlimited liability
• have to make all the decisions alone
• business dies with the founder

A3 • getting finance
• choosing a suitable location
• may take time to build up customers

A4 want independence; lost previous job; see a business opportunity

***examiner's* note** Setting up in business as a sole trader can be exciting and rewarding, but it can also be very stressful.

Partnership

Q1 State two problems of a partnership.

Q2 State one advantage of a partnership over a sole trader.

Q3 What is the equation for market share?

Q4 Give two examples of organisations that are not profit making.

ANSWERS

when two or more individuals trade together in business (under the Partnership Act)

A1 • individuals may disagree over objectives
   • it usually has unlimited liability

A2 ideas and skills can be shared in a partnership; more finance

A3 $$\text{market share (\%)} = \frac{\text{sales of a particular firm or brand}}{\text{total market sales}} \times 100$$

A4 • charity organisations with social objectives, e.g. helping the homeless
   • organisations in the public sector

***examiner's* note** The right form of business organisation depends on the views of those setting it up. Are they willing to share power? Are they willing to have other owners? Is limited liability important?

 **19** ANSWERS

Company

Q1 State one advantage of a public limited company (plc) becoming a private limited company (ltd).

Q2 State two ways in which profit can be used.

Q3 State two other forms of business apart from a company.

Q4 State three causes of cash outflows from a business.

ANSWERS

a business with limited liability that is owned by shareholders

A1 less vulnerable to being bought by a competitor as you can control the sale of shares; less regulation

A2
- to reward shareholders
- retained for investment

A3
- sole trader
- partnership
- cooperative

A4
- to employees
- for rent
- for materials
- to pay interest
- to pay for marketing

***examiner's* note** Most companies in the UK are private limited companies; only a few thousand are public limited companies.

Shareholder

Q1 The amount paid out of profits to shareholders is called a
d.............; the rest is ....

Q2 Why might an investor buy shares?

Q3 If a share increases in price, does the company earn more
money? Why?

Q4 Every shareholder has one vote each. True or false? Why?

ANSWERS ▶▶

A1 dividend; retained (kept)

A2 to gain from the share price increasing later; to receive a dividend; to vote

A3 no; the company only earns money when a share is first sold

A4 false; one vote per share

examiner's note Some shareholders put pressure on managers to provide short-term profits; others are willing to let the firm invest for the future and wait for long-term rewards. The amount a firm pays out in dividends may depend on the amount of profits it has and the pressure from investors for rewards.

(21) ANSWERS

Director

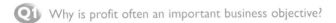

Q1 Why is profit often an important business objective?

Q2 What type of liability does a company have – limited or unlimited?

Q3 Does the government own a public limited company?

Q4 A director must be employed full time by the firm. True or false? Explain.

ANSWERS

person elected by shareholders to represent their interests

A1 can use it to reward owners; can use it to finance growth; likely to affect the share price

A2 limited

A3 no, shareholders do; governments own public corporations

A4 false; a director may be appointed specifically to provide an outside view and need not work full time in the business

***examiner's* note** Sometimes shareholders and managers want different things (e.g. managers may want to keep profits to invest for the future whereas shareholders may want profits paid out immediately). This can lead to conflict between the two groups. Sometimes the shareholders force managers to resign.

Private limited company

Q1 What initials does a private limited company have after its name?

Q2 Who owns a private limited company?

Q3 Are all employees shareholders in a company?

Q4 Are all businesses companies? Explain.

ANSWERS

A1 ltd

A2 shareholders

A3 no; some may be, but certainly not all

A4 no; some are sole traders or partnerships

***examiner's* note** Private limited companies are often (but not always) owned by families. In a private limited company, the owners can control who shares are sold to, e.g. shares can be kept within the family. In a plc, shareholders can sell their shares to whoever they want.

Public limited company

Q1 What initials does a public limited company have after its name?

Q2 Why might a private limited company want to become a public limited company?

Q3 Why might a firm's share price increase?

Q4 State three reasons for an investor buying a share.

ANSWERS

a company that has its shares quoted on the Stock Exchange

A1 plc

A2 to sell shares on the Stock Exchange and have more access to investors; to have a higher profile

A3 higher demand for shares (e.g. shareholders expect the share price, or dividends, to increase)

A4 • to vote
   • to receive a dividend
   • to gain from a share price increase

***examiner's* note** Public limited companies are usually (but not always) bigger than private limited companies.

Limited liability

Q1 Does a sole trader have unlimited liability or limited liability?

Q2 Why is limited liability important to attract investors?

Q3 What determines whether a company can sell more shares?

Q4 State one disadvantage of setting up as a company.

ANSWERS

investors may lose the money invested in the business but not their personal possessions

A1 unlimited

A2 limits what they can lose, so they are more likely to invest

A3 the price; the track record of the company; the future plans of the business

A4 have to pay to have accounts audited; have to publish accounts, so loss of privacy

***examiner's* note** Even with limited liability, investing in companies can be risky. Share prices can fall and companies can be closed down if they are bankrupt. On the other hand, investors may benefit from dividends from the company and from increases in the share price.

Franchise

Q1 What is the difference between a franchisor and a franchisee?

Q2 State two benefits of selling a franchise.

Q3 State two benefits of buying a franchise.

Q4 What is a partnership? Explain the benefit compared to a sole trader.

ANSWERS

when one firm grants another firm the right to supply its products

A1 franchisor sells the franchise; franchisee buys it

A2 • raise revenue
  • grow more quickly
  • sell to people eager to make the business work

A3 • may be an established and proven idea
  • can benefit from ideas and experiences of other franchisees and the franchisor

A4 two or more individuals working together in business; they can share ideas, skills, finance and stress

***examiner's* note** Selling a franchise can be risky because the people buying may not behave in the way you want. Sometimes the sellers have ended up buying them back.

Aims and objectives

Q1 Identify possible objectives of a business.

Q2 The plan to achieve a company's objectives is called the s_____.

Q3 Why do firms want to grow?

Q4 How might the size of a business be measured?

ANSWERS

A1 profits; survival; growth; customer satisfaction; to be environmentally friendly; to be ethical and sustainable

A2 strategy

A3 economies of scale; market power; status; pride and sense of achievement

A4 value of sales (£); volume of sales (number of units); number of employees

***examiner's* note** The objectives of a business will change over time. For example, when starting up the priority of a business may be to survive, later it may focus on growing, and later again it may focus on increasing profitability.

Stakeholders

Q1 Are all stakeholders shareholders?

Q2 An organisation that attempts to get a firm to change its behaviour is called a p................ g................

Q3 State three stakeholders of a firm.

Q4 Give an example of when stakeholders' objectives conflict.

ANSWERS

individuals or groups that are affected by a firm's activities

A1 no; not every stakeholder owns a share in the business

A2 pressure group

A3 • suppliers
   • local community
   • employees
   • distributors
   • government

A4 employees' demands for higher wages may reduce the profits for shareholders; customers want lower prices that may reduce investors' profits

***examiner's* note** More firms have acknowledged the importance of stakeholder groups in recent years. They have realised that cooperating with stakeholders may help them to succeed.

Stakeholder friendly business

Q1 State three stakeholder groups.

Q2 Give an example of how stakeholder objectives might coincide.

Q3 Why is it important to try to meet customer needs?

Q4 Why is it important to meet employee needs?

ANSWERS

describes an organisation that takes into account its stakeholders' needs when making a decision

A1
- employees
- customers
- government
- members of the local community
- suppliers
- investors

A2 providing better quality products for customers may lead to higher sales and ultimately higher profits for shareholders

A3 to generate sales; to attract and keep customers and stop them switching to competitors

A4 to keep them motivated — this affects productivity, absenteeism and how long people stay at a business

examiner's note Many shareholders in the UK are big financial institutions that are looking for quick, high rewards to pay to the people who invested in them.

(29) ANSWERS

Business ethics

Q1 What is a stakeholder?

Q2 What actions can pressure groups take?

Q3 What is social responsibility?

Q4 Identify different areas of business affected by employment laws.

ANSWERS

A1 an individual or organisation that affects and is affected by a firm's activities

A2 they can boycott a business and not buy its products; they can have a publicity campaign to change the firm's behaviour

A3 when a firm accepts obligations to society over and above its legal responsibilities (e.g. to protect the environment, help the community, promote good causes)

A4 recruitment (equal opportunities); dismissal; redundancy; pay (minimum wage); employment rights (e.g. maternity, right to strike, right to join a union, working hours)

***examiner's* note** Ethical behaviour may attract investors and employees who want to be associated with such a firm, but it may mean turning away certain orders.

Unethical behaviour

Q1 State two examples of ethical issues in marketing.

Q2 State two ethical issues to do with production.

Q3 How can business activity affect the environment badly?

Q4 What might happen if a business is found to be behaving unethically?

ANSWERS

A1
- whether to target children
- whether to mislead people to sell more
- whether to encourage people to spend even if they cannot afford it

A2
- whether to cut costs even if safety falls as a result
- whether to use very cheap labour abroad even if workers are not treated well
- what quality to provide

A3 can pollute; can create noise; can lead to congestion; can affect air, noise, water and quality of life of the community

A4 may lead to lower sales; customers may switch away or protest; if illegal it could be sued; investors may not want to invest any more; may lose employees

***examiner's* note** A business has many stakeholders (e.g. customers, employees, investors, suppliers, the community). It may not be possible to meet all their needs but a manager could try to behave fairly.

(31) ANSWERS

External costs

Q1 Give two examples of the external costs a business can generate.

Q2 Why might a business take account of its external costs?

Q3 State two ways in which a business might be environmentally responsible.

Q4 What is a social enterprise?

ANSWERS

costs imposed on society by a firm's actions: social costs = private costs + external costs

A1 • pollution
   • noise
   • congestion

A2 if it wants to behave responsibly; if it is made to by the government (e.g. laws or taxes)

A3 • recycling
   • reusing
   • reducing wastage and emissions

A4 a business set up to help society rather than to make a profit

***examiner's* note** The actions of businesses affect society and the environment. Some managers may consider such effects when deciding on their actions; others may focus purely on profit.

SWOT analysis

Q1 State two possible marketing strengths.

Q2 Are strengths and weaknesses internal or external?

Q3 Is a forecasted fall in the market size an opportunity or threat? Why?

Q4 What is a strategy?

ANSWERS

examines the strengths and weaknesses
of a business and the opportunities
and threats it faces to develop a strategy

A1 • strong brand
   • widespread distribution
   • distinctive product
   • USP
   • broad portfolio of products

A2 internal — they refer to the current position of a business

A3 a threat because firms will have to fight harder for sales

A4 a long-term plan to achieve an objective

***examiner's* note** SWOT analysis helps to plan but does not guarantee that
the right plan is chosen or that it can be put into action effectively.

 33 ANSWERS

Business growth

Q1 State two ways of measuring the size of a business.

Q2 State two ways in a business might expand.

Q3 State two reasons why a business might want to grow.

Q4 What are the possible problems for a business of expanding?

ANSWERS

occurs when an organisation increases in size (e.g. sales increase)

A1 • sales (volume or value)   • number of outlets
    • number of employees   • value of the business

A2 • organic (internal) growth
    • external growth (e.g. merger or takeover)
    • selling franchises

A3 • to gain economies of scale   • to gain market power
    • to gain market share   • for status

A4 problems of control, communication and coordination leading to diseconomies of scale

examiner's note There are advantages in growing but businesses must avoid becoming too big as they may become inefficient. Managers need to think about how to manage the process of growth.

Takeover

Q1 When two firms join together this is called a m...............

Q2 Why might firms want to join together?

Q3 If a firm gets too big, unit costs may increase due to d...............
of s...............

Q4 If one firm sells the right to use its name and products to
another, this is called f...............

ANSWERS

A1 merger

A2 share resources; economies of scale

A3 diseconomies of scale

A4 franchise

***examiner's* note** Integration can provide a quick means of growth, although this can also cause problems of control, coordination and motivation. Firms may decide to join with other businesses for various reasons. They may join with suppliers to secure supplies; they may join with distributors to ensure access to markets; they may join with competitors to gain market share.

Marketing

Q1 What is meant by a market-oriented firm?

Q2 State two factors that might influence product design.

Q3 The model that shows sales of a product over time is called the p.............. l...... c...........

Q4 The gathering of information for marketing is called m.................... r....................

ANSWERS

A1 a business that bases decisions on what customers want

A2 costs of production; look of the product; how product will be used; target audience; overall brand

A3 product life cycle

A4 market research

***examiner's* note** Effective marketing has become increasingly important given ever-greater levels of competition and choice for the customer. Marketing involves understanding customer needs, deciding which segment(s) to target and implementing an effective marketing mix.

Demand

Q1 State three reasons why demand for a product may increase.

Q2 Managers use the marketing mix to influence demand. What are the elements of the marketing mix?

Q3 What might be the effect of an increase in demand for a product on the price of that product?

Q4 What is the difference between a customer and a consumer?

ANSWERS

how much of a product customers are willing and able to buy

A1 • more buyers in the market
   • more income for consumers
   • fewer substitutes
   • better marketing

A2 price, place, product, promotion

A3 the price is likely to increase because people want it and will be willing to pay more to get it

A4 a customer buys the product; a consumer uses the product (e.g. a parent may be the customer buying a toy for his or her child, the consumer)

***examiner's* note** Demand can change suddenly for some products: films can be popular for a few weeks and then demand falls; certain toys and bands can be very popular for several months and then go out of fashion.

Market research

Q1 Distinguish between primary (field) and secondary (desk) research.

Q2 State three benefits of market research.

Q3 How much should a firm spend on market research?

Q4 Would you use primary (field) or secondary (desk) research to test a new product idea? Why?

ANSWERS

A1 primary gathers new data; secondary uses data that already exist

A2 • more focused marketing
  • less waste of marketing effort
  • less risk in decision making
  • can identify opportunities
  • can review marketing activities

A3 depends on how much it has, what it is trying to find out and the expected returns

A4 primary; the idea is new so there are no previous data

***examiner's* note** Market research can help a firm to make better decisions, but it cannot guarantee success.

Market share

Q1 State three reasons why a firm's market share might fall.

Q2 A firm's market share is 20% and its sales are £30,000.
What is the total market value?

Q3 State two factors that might determine the size of a firm's
promotional budget.

Q4 State the benefits to a manufacturer of having a bigger
market share.

ANSWERS

sales of a product as a percentage of total sales in the market

A1 • poor marketing
   • poor quality product
   • competitors' actions
   • change in fashion/tastes

A2 1% = 30,000/20 = £1,500; 100% = 100 × £1,500 = £150,000

A3 • marketing objectives
   • financial resources
   • how responsive demand is to promotional spending
   • what competitors are spending

A4 power over retailers; possible economies of scale; greater brand awareness, making it easier to launch new products

***examiner's* note** More market share does not always mean more sales. It is possible to have a bigger share of a smaller market with fewer sales.

Market segments

Q1 One firm's sales as a percentage of the whole market are called its m............... s...............

Q2 How might the size of a market be measured?

Q3 Identify different ways of segmenting a market with examples.

Q4 State one advantage of segmenting a market.

ANSWERS

groups of similar needs and wants within a market

A1 market share

A2 by the number of items sold (volume); by the value of the items sold

A3 age (e.g. toys); gender (e.g. clothes); income (e.g. housing); region (e.g. local newspapers); lifestyle (e.g. single or family); socioeconomic group (e.g. senior manager, manual worker)

A4 can amend the marketing mix appropriately for different segments so more effective marketing

***examiner's* note** With more competition in markets nowadays, firms are targeting ever more segments. Think of how many different types of shampoo there are. More competition means that firms need to be more market oriented. Unless they meet customer needs precisely, they will lose sales to their rivals.

Product life cycle

Q1 State the stages of the product life cycle.

Q2 Attempts to keep sales increasing and to avoid decline are called e................... s....................

Q3 State four reasons why sales may decline.

Q4 What would you expect to happen to cash flow in the early stages of the life cycle? Why?

ANSWERS ❯❯

shows how sales of a product change over time

A1 development, introduction, growth, maturity and decline

A2 extension strategies

A3 • new competitors
   • new technology
   • failure to update marketing
   • changing tastes

A4 likely to be negative; sales are low and the product needs promoting extensively

***examiner's* note** The problem with the product life cycle model is that it is often only possible to tell what stage a product is at much later on. A fall in sales may be because the product is in the decline stage or may simply be a temporary reduction – you can only tell much later.

Extension strategies

Q1 What are on the axes of a diagram to show the product life cycle?

Q2 What is the maturity phase of the product life cycle?

Q3 If sales were £25,000 and increased to £30,000, what is the percentage growth?

Q4 If sales growth is negative, what stage of the life cycle is the business in?

ANSWERS

A1 sales and time

A2 occurs when sales are growing slowly

A3 percentage change $= \dfrac{\text{change}}{\text{original}} \times 100 = \dfrac{£5,000}{£25,000} \times 100 = 20\%$

A4 this means sales are falling, so it is the decline stage

examiner's note In some cases it may too expensive or too difficult to try and prolong the life cycle with extension strategies, so the business may focus on developing new products instead.

Product portfolio

Q1 Why should a business analyse its product portfolio?

Q2 Why might a business want to sell several products?

Q3 Why is new product development difficult?

Q4 What is a market segment?

ANSWERS

the collection of products that a business provides

A1 to see what to do next (e.g. develop new products or stop producing some existing ones)

A2 to meet needs of different segments; to spread risks; to enter more markets

A3 can be expensive; many new products fail due to competition or poor market research; may involve new technology

A4 small group of similar needs and wants within the overall market

***examiner's* note** Managing a range of products can be difficult because they may face different competitors and operate in different markets; however, having several products may enable the business to grow faster.

Marketing mix

Q1 What are the four elements of the marketing mix?

Q2 State three factors that might influence how much is spent by a firm on advertising.

Q3 Give examples of types of promotion in marketing.

Q4 How might a firm react to a fall in sales?

ANSWERS ▶▶

A1 • price • place • promotion • product

A2 • the firm's overall financial resources
• its marketing objectives
• which advertising media are used

A3 price cuts; special offers; point-of-sale displays; free samples; competitions; after-sales service; advertising

A4 increase promotional activities; cut prices; modify the product

***examiner's* note** The importance of the elements of the mix will vary from product to product and from time to time. In a recession, people may be more sensitive to price. Demand for cars is more sensitive to television advertising than demand for pencils.

Penetration pricing

Q1 State two factors that might influence the price of a product.

Q2 What is price skimming?

Q3 What is predatory pricing?

Q4 What is a loss leader?

ANSWERS

A1 • costs
   • degree of competition
   • demand
   • objectives
   • competitors' prices
   • pricing strategy

A2 setting a high price for innovative products to enter a market

A3 lowering the price below costs to try and force competitors out of a market

A4 a low promotional price on some items to attract customers into the store to buy other products

***examiner's* note** The price can have a big impact on demand and the sales of the business and therefore its profits.

45 ANSWERS

Promotion

Q1 The four Ps are know as the m................ m............ .

Q2 State two reasons for lowering the price of an item.

Q3 State two ways of promoting a business.

Q4 State four determinants of the type of advertising selected by a firm.

ANSWERS

A1 marketing mix

A2 • to boost sales
    • because competitors have lowered their price

A3 small-budget promotions: advertising in local newspapers, the internet, personal recommendation, business cards; larger-budget promotions: more advertising, sponsorship, public relations

A4 • the number of people it reaches
    • costs
    • composition of audience (e.g. age, income)
    • the nature of the product or service

examiner's note The different elements of the marketing mix must work together (e.g. a heavily branded product sold in exclusive outlets is likely to have a high price).

Promotional activities

Q1 State two ways of promoting a product.

Q2 State three factors that might determine how much is spent on promotion.

Q3 State two types of promotional message.

Q4 Give three examples of sales promotions.

ANSWERS

ways of communicating about a business and its products

A1 • advertising
   • sales force
           • sales promotions
           • PR

A2 • the media used
    • the firm's objectives
    • the firm's resources

A3 remind customers about a product; make them aware of it; inform customers; persuade customers to buy

A4 • buy one, get one free
    • short-term discounts
    • competitions

***examiner's* note** Promotional activities may be undertaken for different reasons (e.g. to inform people that a new product is available, to persuade them that one brand is better than another or to reassure them that they have made the right decision).

Distribution channel

Q1 What is a retailer?

Q2 State two factors that influence a firm's choice of distribution channel.

Q3 Identify two problems of selling via intermediaries.

Q4 Apart from using retailers, name two other channels of distribution.

ANSWERS ▶▶

A1 a business selling a final product. Types of retailer include department store, independent retailer, hypermarket, chain store.

A2 costs; coverage of the market; target audience and where it is located; desire for control over the final price and promotion; nature of the product

A3 • no control over final price
- no control over the way products are sold and promoted in the shops
- intermediaries add on a profit margin

A4 • wholesalers
- telesales
- mail order
- internet selling

***examiner's* note** With the internet, the trend has been towards more direct distribution, selling direct to the consumer.

New product development

Q1 Modifying an existing product might keep its sales going. This is an e_____ s_____.

Q2 State five stages of the product life cycle.

Q3 State two reasons why so many new products fail.

Q4 Why might firms need to invest in new products?

ANSWERS ▶

producing new products to launch on the market

A1 extension strategy

A2 development, introduction, growth, maturity and decline

A3 • poor market research   • problems with quality
     • competitors' actions   • poor marketing

A4 because of the need to keep up with competitors; because customers want new products; because of new technology

examiner's **note** Investing in new product development is risky because many new products fail, but in many industries such investment is essential for long-term success.

e-commerce

Q1 What is the internet?

Q2 How can the internet help businesses?

Q3 What factors might a manufacturer consider before selling directly via the internet?

Q4 What are the advantages and disadvantages of e-commerce?

ANSWERS ▶▶

the buying and selling of goods and services over the internet

A1 worldwide online network accessed by computer

A2 can market their products; can use the internet to find information

A3 reaction of its existing retailers; impact on price; security for payment; initial design costs for a website; how to get products to customers

A4 *Advantages:* relatively cheap to set up – do not need expensive locations; access to global markets
Disadvantages: customers cannot see the products directly; they may worry about security when they pay; they may be encouraged to 'shop around'

***examiner's* note** e-commerce is a major growth area, with many businesses appreciating the appeal of selling via the internet. However, not all succeed and some businesses operating purely on the internet have found it difficult to make a profit.

Sources of finance

Q1 State two ways in which a firm can raise money from outside the business, apart from selling shares.

Q2 State two ways in which a firm can raise money from within the business.

Q3 Is issuing shares a short- or long-term source of finance?

Q4 Give an example of a profitability ratio.

ANSWERS

A1 • overdraft
  • loans

A2 • sale of assets
  • profits

A3 long-term

A4 return on capital employed or profit margin

***examiner's* note** Raising finance can be particularly difficult for new businesses because they do not have a track record and usually have relatively few assets.

Loan

Q1 State one problem of borrowing money.

Q2 State one disadvantage of selling more shares to raise finance.

Q3 What is the difference between a plc and an ltd?

Q4 Who owns a business in the public sector?

ANSWERS

A1 have to pay interest

A2 have to bring in new owners, lose control as they have a vote

A3 a plc can advertise its shares and sell them on the Stock Exchange

A4 the government

***examiner's* note** Borrowing money can make good business sense provided a firm can earn more with the money than it has to pay back. Before deciding whether to borrow money a firm may consider how much it has already borrowed, the interest rate and the length of time it has to repay the loan.

Net cash flow

Q1 How can a business improve its cash flow?

Q2 Current assets are £3,000; current liabilities are £1,000; stocks are £1,500. What is the current ratio?

Q3 Current assets are £3,000; current liabilities are £1,000; stocks are £1,500. What is the acid test ratio?

Q4 How can a business sell an item but not receive cash immediately?

ANSWERS

the difference between the inflows and outflows of cash of the business

A1 chase money owed to it; insist on cash being paid for items; delay paying suppliers; take out an overdraft

A2 current ratio = current assets/current liabilities = £3,000/£1,000 = 3

A3 acid test ratio = (current assets − stock)/current liabilities = (£3,000 − £1,500)/£1,000 = 1.5

A4 if it sells on credit

examiner's note A business must ensure it has enough cash to pay its bills or it will not survive.

Cash-flow forecasting

Q1 State one reason for producing a cash-flow forecast.

Q2 State three reasons why a cash-flow forecast might be wrong.

Q3 What happens if a firm has too little cash?

Q4 State two ways in which a firm might increase its cash flow quickly.

ANSWERS

estimating future inflows and outflows of cash

A1 to estimate when a firm may have cash-flow problems and needs to borrow money

A2 • customers may be slower to pay than expected
   • suppliers may demand payment more quickly than expected
   • sales may be lower than expected

A3 may not be able to pay bills so may be closed down; lacks liquidity

A4 • arrange an overdraft
   • sell stocks cheaply
   • chase debtors

***examiner's* note** When firms grow they often have cash-flow problems because they are spending so much to buy the equipment, stocks and facilities in advance.

 ANSWERS

Profit and loss account

Q1 What is meant by gross profit?

Q2 What is the difference between gross profit and net profit?

Q3 If the net profit margin is 5% and sales are £40,000, what are net profits?

Q4 If gross profits are increasing but net profits are falling, what is happening?

ANSWERS

shows the income and costs of a business over a year

A1 revenue minus the costs of sales (i.e. the costs of directly supplying the product)

A2 net profit = gross profit − overheads (also called expenses)

A3 £40,000 × (5/100) = £2,000

A4 overheads (e.g. administration costs, managers' salaries and interest on loans) must be increasing, bringing down the net profit

***examiner's* note** Making a profit is often an objective of a business; profits can be used to invest in a business or reward owners. Other objectives may be to grow, to provide a service for society, to survive or to help stakeholders.

Revenue

Q1 Sales of product A are £40,000. The market size is £200,000. What is the market share of the product?

Q2 A firm has a 25% market share of a market worth £120,000. What are its sales worth?

Q3 State two advantages to a firm of having a high level of brand loyalty.

Q4 How can a firm increase its sales?

ANSWERS

A1 $\dfrac{£40,000}{£200,000} \times 100 = 20\%$

A2 $£120,000 \times \dfrac{25}{100} = £30,000$

A3 • may be able to charge more
   • can introduce new products more easily

A4 promote its products more; cut prices; improve distribution

***examiner's* note** Boosting revenue is not enough in itself. A company may do this by spending so much on advertising that its profits fall!

Costs

Q1 Costs are £3,000; profit is £4,000. What is the firm's revenue?

Q2 Unit costs are £50; output is 30 units. What are total costs?

Q3 What is a fixed cost? Give an example.

Q4 What is a variable cost? Give an example.

ANSWERS

the value of items used up by the business in the accounting period

A1 £7,000

A2 £1,500

A3 a cost that does not change with output, e.g. rent

A4 a cost that changes with output, e.g. material costs

***examiner's* note** Cutting costs is not always a good idea. Sometimes it can mean that quality suffers and demand falls. If, however, sales are maintained, lower costs will mean higher profits. These profits may be paid out to the owners or used for investment.

Loss

Q1 State two types of cost. Explain the difference.

Q2 If fixed costs increase, does breakeven output increase or decrease? Why?

Q3 If the selling price increases, does breakeven output increase or decrease? Why?

Q4 State two assumptions of breakeven analysis.

ANSWERS

A1 • fixed costs: do not change with output
   • variable costs: do change with output

A2 increase — need to sell more to cover the higher costs

A3 decrease — less has to be sold to cover costs

A4 • all units are sold at the same price
   • all units produced are sold
   • the variable cost per unit is constant

examiner's note Breakeven analysis can be helpful to new firms that want to estimate whether or not they are likely to make a profit with their idea.

Profitability

Q1 What is meant by a gross profit margin?

Q2 State three measures of a firm's success, apart from profit.

Q3 When does a loss occur?

Q4 What is meant by net profit?

ANSWERS

the profit that a firm makes in relation to its sales or capital employed

A1 profit per sale; $\left(\dfrac{\text{gross profit}}{\text{sales}}\right) \times 100$

A2
- growth
- sales
- number of employees
- market share
- number of outlets
- meeting social objectives

A3 when costs are higher than revenue

A4 revenue − cost of sales = gross profit
gross profit − expenses = net profit

***examiner's* note** Not every organisation aims to be profitable (e.g. charities, libraries and the National Health Service). Some firms may sacrifice short-term profit for other objectives, e.g. by cutting price they may gain market share; by investing in new products they may attract new customers.

Gross profit

Q1 What is the difference between gross and net profit?

Q2 What is the difference between an asset and a liability?

Q3 Net profit is £300 and total revenue is £700. What are total costs?

Q4 Why does a firm want to make a profit?

ANSWERS

sales revenue minus the cost of sales

A1 net profit deducts overheads and expenses (e.g. administration and marketing) from gross profit

A2 an asset is owned by a firm; a liability is owed by a firm

A3 net profit = revenue − total costs
£300 = £700 − total costs
total costs = £400

A4 to generate funds for investment and expansion; to reward the owners

***examiner's* note** When examining a firm's accounts, it is important to put the figures in context by considering past figures and the figures of competitors.

Breakeven

Q1 What is the title of the line Y?

Q2 What is the breakeven output?

Q3 How much profit is made at an output of 30 units?

Q4 What are the fixed costs?

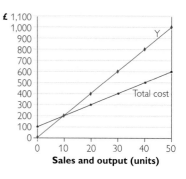

ANSWERS

A1 total revenue

A2 10 units; this is the output at which total revenue = total costs

A3 £200

A4 £100

***examiner's* note** A breakeven chart shows the profit or loss at any level of output. At levels of output below breakeven the firm makes a loss. At output levels above breakeven the firm makes a profit. The difficulty is forecasting what the actual level of sales will be.

Balance sheet

Q1 What is an asset?

Q2 What is a current liability?

Q3 Which of the following is an asset: overdraft, loan, stock or creditor?

Q4 What is a limitation of a balance sheet?

ANSWERS

shows the financial position of a firm at a particular moment in time

A1 something the firm owns

A2 something that has to be paid by the firm within a year

A3 stock

A4 only shows the position at a given moment – it is likely to be out of date and may not help predict the future

***examiner's* note** Companies have to produce financial accounts each year. These include a balance sheet and a profit and loss statement. These accounts will be of interest to various stakeholder groups such as employees, investors, suppliers and the government.

Current assets

Q1 What is the equation for the current ratio?

Q2 What is the equation for the acid test ratio?

Q3 What does a low acid test ratio suggest?

Q4 To be liquid, should current assets be higher or lower than current liabilities?

ANSWERS

A1   current assets
     current liabilities

A2   current assets − stock
      current liabilities

A3 liquidity problems

A4 higher

***examiner's* note** Being liquid is not in itself enough for most firms. It simply means that the firm can pay its bills. Most firms want to be profitable as well.

Liquidity

Q1 What is meant by a current liability?

Q2 What is a current asset?

Q3 What does an acid test ratio of 0.1 tell you about a business?

Q4 Current assets are £500; current liabilities are £300.
What is the current ratio?

ANSWERS

A1 money that is owed in the short term

A2 something a firm owns that can be turned into cash within a year

A3 business may have liquidity problems because stocks and cash are
only 10% of the current liabilities

A4 $\dfrac{500}{300} = 1.6667$

***examiner's* note** Being liquid means that a firm can meet its current liabilities.
Firms usually want to be profitable as well. If a firm has liquidity problems, it may
try to borrow money. However, banks may be reluctant to lend in case they lose
their money.

Organisational chart

Q1 In the diagram shown, what is the span of control?

Q2 What is the number of levels of hierarchy?

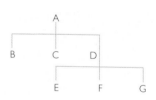

Q3 Is the chain of command ECB, FDC, ADG or BCD?

Q4 Can you tell if the organisation is centralised or decentralised?

ANSWERS

A1 3 people

A2 2 levels

A3 ADG

A4 cannot tell – the chart does not show the extent to which authority is retained at the top of the organisation

examiner's **note** An organisational chart shows who reports to whom, but does not show the amount of authority each individual position has (e.g. how much spending it controls). However, the chart will show how jobs are organised, e.g. whether jobs are grouped geographically, by function or by product.

Span of control

Q1 State two factors influencing the span of control.

Q2 State one possible problem if the span of control is too wide.

Q3 What is meant by a level of hierarchy?

Q4 What is meant by the chain of command?

ANSWERS

A1 • the nature of the task
   • the ability and nature of superior and subordinate

A2 manager has too little time for the subordinates

A3 a level of responsibility within the organisation

A4 the vertical line of authority within a business (e.g. A has authority over B, who has authority over C etc.)

***examiner's* note** If the structure of an organisation is wrong, this can mean that decision making is slow and that costs increase.

Levels of hierarchy

Q1 If the span of control increases, what is likely to happen to the number of levels of hierarchy?

Q2 If you accept that it is your job to complete a task, then you accept r................................ for this task.

Q3 What problems might there be if a firm has many levels of hierarchy?

Q4 What advantages are there of having many levels of hierarchy?

ANSWERS

A1 likely to reduce – will not need so many people to supervise employees

A2 responsibility

A3 slow communication; messages may be distorted going from top to bottom as there are many intermediaries

A4 many promotion opportunities; possibly small spans of control

examiner's note An organisational chart shows who reports to whom. It does not show how much authority someone has.

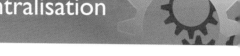

Centralisation

Q1 State two advantages of centralisation.

Q2 What is the opposite of centralisation?

Q3 State one disadvantage of centralisation.

Q4 Buying all the supplies for an organisation from one office can lead to bulk discounts. This is a purchasing e_____ of s_____. Name three other types.

ANSWERS

when authority within an organisation is kept by a small number of senior managers

A1 • decision makers have an overview of the business
   • it leads to consistency across the business

A2 decentralisation

A3 may mean that managers cannot react to local conditions or that local managers are demoralised as they cannot make decisions for themselves

A4 economy of scale; technical, financial, managerial

***examiner's* note** Centralisation becomes more difficult the bigger a firm gets, the more regions it operates in and the more products it offers because there is more to control.

Management style

Q1 What is an authoritarian manager?

Q2 What is a democratic manager?

Q3 A company is always owned by its managers. True or false?

Q4 A sole trader is the owner and the manager of a business. True or false?

ANSWERS ▶▶

A1 a manager who tells people what to do

A2 a manager who listens to employees before making a decision

A3 false; companies are owned by shareholders

A4 true, which is why it can be quite stressful

***examiner's* note** A good manager is one element in the success of a firm. Success also depends on the employees, the product itself, the competition and the economy. A manager must be able to plan, organise, coordinate and control people and activities.

Delegation

Q1 State three benefits of delegation.

Q2 State one disadvantage of delegation.

Q3 State two conditions necessary for effective delegation.

Q4 If senior managers refuse to delegate and keep all authority themselves, the organisation will be very c............................

ANSWERS

A1 • motivates staff
   • firm benefits from the skills of others
   • frees up superiors' time

A2 • superiors lose control of decisions
   • subordinates may lack necessary skills

A3 • subordinates must know exactly what to do
   • they must have the necessary resources

A4 centralised

***examiner's* note** The amount of delegation in an organisation depends on the managers' willingness to give up some control and the willingness of subordinates to accept responsibility.

Communication

Q1 State three benefits of good communication in a business.

Q2 State three barriers to communication in a large business.

Q3 State three consequences of poor communication in a firm.

Q4 Are many layers of hierarchy likely to improve or worsen communication? Why?

ANSWERS

A1 • may motivate staff   • better decisions
   • keep in touch with customers

A2 • too many layers of hierarchy   • cultural differences
   • conflicting objectives   • lack of IT

A3 • poor decision making   • demotivated employees
   • lack of direction   • no common sense of purpose

A4 worsen; messages have to pass through more layers and may be distorted and delayed

***examiner's* note** Communication is important within the business (e.g. with employees) and with groups outside the business (e.g. with potential investors).

Recruitment

Q1 State one advantage of internal recruitment.

Q2 Distinguish between a job description and a job (or person) specification.

Q3 What is the difference between internal and external recruitment?

Q4 What is meant by staff retention?

ANSWERS

the process of attracting applicants to a job vacancy

A1 managers know the people already and are aware of strengths and past performance

A2 a job description sets out what the job entails; a job (or person) specification sets out the requirements needed by someone to do the job

A3 internal recruitment means recruiting from within the business; external recruitment means recruiting from outside the business

A4 measures how long staff stay with the business once recruited

examiner's **note** How easy it is to recruit for a position depends on the nature of the job and the labour market (e.g. how many people are looking for a job).

(72) ANSWERS

Selection

Q1 What is induction training?

Q2 State three items that may be on a person's application for a job.

Q3 State two factors which are important in conducting an effective interview.

Q4 State two benefits of training.

ANSWERS

the process of deciding which applicant for a job to accept

A1 introduces employees to the job, the organisation and their colleagues

A2 • previous experience • qualifications • age • skills

A3 • giving the interviewee the opportunity to talk
  • ensuring that there are no unwanted interruptions

A4 • may lead to higher productivity
  • employees may be more highly motivated and more willing to stay at the business
  • increase skills

***examiner's* note** Poor selection processes are likely to lead to staff leaving quickly, mistakes occurring and training being expensive.

Remuneration

Q1 What is a salary?

Q2 What is a pension?

Q3 What is piece-rate? State one advantage and one disadvantage of this payment system.

Q4 What is a bonus?

ANSWERS ▶▶

A1 a fixed sum per year, paid monthly to employees

A2 a payment to employees once they have retired

A3 payment by output; encourages more production, but quality may suffer

A4 additional payment on top of normal pay, e.g. for hitting sales budgets

***examiner's* note** Financial rewards may motivate staff, but in many cases employees are more motivated by the job itself, the feedback they receive and the degree of authority they have. The extent to which money motivates staff depends on how much they are paid, whether the rewards are linked to effort, and whether staff know what they are supposed to do to increase their earnings.

Non-monetary benefits

Q1 Name two non-monetary benefits.

Q2 Name two monetary benefits a business might offer employees in addition to the basic earnings.

Q3 What else affects the amount someone produces as well as their motivation?

Q4 How can the way a job is designed affect motivation?

ANSWERS

ways of rewarding people without paying more

A1 • longer holidays
- bigger office
- fringe benefits (e.g. free lunches, office parties, flexible hours)

A2 • pensions
- profit sharing
- bonuses

A3 training; equipment; the way the work is organised; basic ability

A4 employees may be motivated by delegation, more authority, better feedback, having a clear role to play in the success of the business

***examiner's* note** Motivating a workforce can be difficult because different people want different things; simply paying more can be expensive and lead to more demands for money, so managers should also look at non-monetary rewards.

 ANSWERS

Training

Q1 State two types of training.

Q2 State two benefits of training.

Q3 State two problems of training.

Q4 What is on-the-job training?

ANSWERS

work-related education to develop skills, attitudes and understanding

A1 • induction
   • on-the-job
   • off-the-job

A2 • increases skills of staff
   • may motivate staff
   • increase productivity
   • helps employees understand better

A3 • costs
   • staff may leave once they have been trained so the company loses the investment

A4 employees are trained as they do the work

***examiner's* note** The amount a firm invests in training depends on the skills needed compared to the skills and finance available.

Induction training

Q1 State three benefits of training.

Q2 State three reasons why firms might not train staff.

Q3 State three factors that influence how much should be spent on training.

Q4 State three ways in which a firm might choose between recruits.

ANSWERS

introducing new recruits to the business and their job

A1 • improve motivation
   • increase productivity
   • improve quality
   • reduce errors
   • improve understanding

A2 • may not need to
   • fear staff may then be recruited by others
   • cost

A3 • funds available
   • skills available compared to skills required
   • need to change attitudes and skills

A4 • interview
   • looking at application forms
   • tests (e.g. physical or intelligence)

***examiner's* note** Training is an investment. Firms must consider the expected benefits compared to the costs before going ahead.

(77) ANSWERS

Trade union

Q1 State three possible forms of industrial action.

Q2 How can a trade union help employees?

Q3 What is collective bargaining?

Q4 State three benefits of better relations between managers and employees.

ANSWERS

an organisation that represents employees' interests at work

A1 • strike • go-slow • work to rule

A2 gives them more power; provides them with expertise and experience to help protect jobs and earnings

A3 when an individual represents a group of other employees when negotiating with management

A4 • higher motivation
• higher productivity
• easier to make changes in the workplace
• employees stay longer
• employees suggest improvements

***examiner's* note** Trade unions have become less popular in the last 10 years in the UK but still provide an important pressure group for protecting jobs and wages, preventing exploitation and helping ensure that the workplace is safe.

Motivation

Q1 State two benefits of a motivated workforce.

Q2 State two ways of motivating staff.

Q3 What is an appraisal?

Q4 What are the problems of a poor retention of staff?

ANSWERS

the desire of individuals to behave in a certain way

A1 • higher productivity
   • more likely to turn up for work

A2 more training; greater authority; delegation; appropriate remuneration; better job design

A3 the superior and subordinate meet to review the subordinate's performance and agree targets for the future

A4 expensive as the business needs to recruit to fill the vacancies; disruptive if people keep leaving; may demotivate those who are left

***examiner's* note** A motivated workforce is not enough to ensure high levels of production. This also depends on technology and the equipment available.

79 ANSWERS

Maslow

Q1 State the needs in Maslow's hierarchy from lowest to highest.

Q2 According to Maslow, what motivates an employee?

Q3 How might a firm meet an employee's security needs?

Q4 How might a firm meet the highest need of employees?

ANSWERS

A1 physiological (basic), security (safety), social, ego (esteem), self-actualisation

A2 depends on where they are in the hierarchy; an employee is motivated by the next level of need, which is not fulfilled at the moment

A3 offer a long-term job contract; ensure a large payout if redundancies are made

A4 by delegating or giving more opportunity for decision making, enabling individuals to take more control of their work

***examiner's* note** Motivating employees can be important in terms of their productivity, their attendance and the quality of their work. Motivation is likely to involve a combination of rewards. Some may be financial, others may include praise, greater responsibility and feedback on performance.

Production

Q1 What is batch production? State one advantage and one disadvantage.

Q2 What is flow production? State one advantage and one disadvantage.

Q3 What is job production? State one advantage and one disadvantage.

Q4 State three objectives of production management.

ANSWERS

the transformation of inputs into outputs

A1 groups of items move from one stage of production to the next; more flexible than flow production, but less flexible than job production

A2 items move continuously along the process; high volume and low unit cost, but inflexible

A3 produces one-off items; flexible, but expensive

A4 • control quality
   • control costs
   • ensure the right volume of production
   • increase efficiency (reduce cost per unit)

***examiner's* note** Production often needs to be flexible and responsive to customer needs. The problem is that this is more expensive than producing large volumes of the same product.

 ANSWERS

Location

Q1 Is rent a fixed or a variable cost? Why?

Q2 When deciding where to locate, a firm will consider breakeven. Define breakeven.

Q3 State two ways in which the government might influence a firm's location.

Q4 What factors might influence the location of a business apart from the government?

ANSWERS

the place where a firm produces

A1 fixed; it does not change with output

A2 the minimum level of output at which revenue equals costs

A3 • offering subsidies or tax cuts
    • controlling planning permission

A4 costs; where the customers are; availability of labour

examiner's note The importance of location varies from business to business. It is vital for a shop or a hotel; it may be less important for the headquarters of an internet bank. Choosing the right location involves a consideration of the costs involved, the possible impact on staff (e.g. how accessible the location is), the availability of supplies and the possible impact on demand.

Capacity

Q1 State three examples of decisions made by a production manager.

Q2 State four ways in which technology might help a firm.

Q3 Explain one advantage and one disadvantage of job production compared to batch.

Q4 Why is it important to be efficient?

ANSWERS

the maximum a firm can produce with its existing resources

A1 • how much to produce
   • how to produce
   • how many stocks to hold
   • where to locate

A2 • keeps costs down
   • produces items quickly
   • produces higher volume
   • produces good-quality products
   • produces a wider range of goods

A3 job production is more flexible; items can be tailor made; but it is often expensive

A4 to keep costs down so the business can be competitive and offer better value for money

examiner's note To increase its capacity a firm might need to invest in new machines and buildings, and to recruit new staff.

Economies of scale

Q1 State three types of economy of scale.

Q2 State one benefit of economies of scale.

Q3 Total costs £20,000; output 400 units. What is the unit cost?

Q4 Unit cost £40; output 200 units. What are total costs?

ANSWERS

occur when unit costs fall as the scale of production increases

A1 • purchasing
   • technical
   • managerial
   • financial

A2 may be able to reduce prices or benefit from higher profit margins

A3 £50

A4 £8,000 (£40 per unit × 200 = £8,000)

***examiner's* note** Economies of scale occur when unit costs fall; total costs are still increasing. With lower unit costs a firm can cut price or maintain price and benefit from higher profit margins.

Diseconomies of scale

Q1 State two diseconomies of scale.

Q2 State two problems of diseconomies of scale.

Q3 As a firm expands from 50 units to 60 units, the unit cost increases to £80. What are the total costs at 60 units?

Q4 If unit costs fall as output expands, this is called an e...................... of s....................

ANSWERS

occur when unit costs increase as the scale of production increases

A1 • problems controlling and coordinating a business
   • employees may be demotivated as they do not feel part of a large business

A2 • may have to increase prices to cover higher unit cost
   • profit margins may fall

A3 £4,800 (£80 per unit × 60 = £4,800)

A4 economy of scale

***examiner's* note** Changing the scale of production may involve purchasing new equipment, finding new facilities and recruiting new staff.

Stocks

Q1 The money invested in stocks could be invested elsewhere. This is called an o................ c................

Q2 Are stocks an asset or a liability of a business? Why?

Q3 State two problems if a firm runs out of stocks.

Q4 What might determine how much stock a firm holds?

ANSWERS ▶▶

materials, components, semi-finished and finished goods held by a firm for use in production or for sale

A1 opportunity cost

A2 an asset; the firm owns them

A3 • cannot produce and therefore cannot meet customer orders
   • may lose sales and goodwill

A4 whether it is using lean production; the warehousing space available for holding stock; demand and rate of usage; opportunity costs

***examiner's* note** The amount of stock held varies greatly from one type of business to another. Manufacturers usually hold more stocks than service firms.

Stock control

Q1 Give examples of types of stock.

Q2 State two factors that influence the level of stocks that a firm holds.

Q3 State four costs of holding stock.

Q4 Why does holding stock involve an opportunity cost?

ANSWERS

A1 raw materials, components, works in progress, finished goods, general supplies

A2 • expected demand
• warehousing costs
• opportunity costs
• reliability of suppliers

A3 • warehousing
• security
• opportunity costs
• depreciation

A4 money could be invested elsewhere (e.g. in a bank)

examiner's note If firms adopt lean production techniques, the stocks they hold should decrease.

Division of labour

Q1 State one benefit of the division of labour.

Q2 State one problem of the division of labour.

Q3 How could a firm try to keep employees who are thinking of leaving?

Q4 Division of labour can help reduce unit costs as output expands. This is an e................. of s.................

ANSWERS

where individual employees are given specialist tasks to undertake in the production process

A1 employees become more productive through repetition; increases efficiency

A2 may lead to boredom and people leaving the business

A3 offer higher wages; better working conditions; more opportunities to be involved

A4 economy of scale

***examiner's* note** The trend in recent years has been towards more teamwork in the workplace rather than the division of labour. Many firms believe that by working in teams employees are more motivated, and the team will come up with more creative solutions.

Quality

Q1 State two benefits of improving quality.

Q2 State two ways of improving quality.

Q3 Why is better quality more important nowadays?

Q4 What is quality control?

ANSWERS

occurs when the product meets customer requirements and is fit for purpose

A1
- fewer rejects and less wastage
- greater customer satisfaction
- greater consistency

A2
- better supplies
- making employees more responsible for their own work
- quality assurance processes to prevent errors
- total quality management — everyone responsible for quality and checking own work

A3 because of more competition and greater demands from customers

A4 inspection of items to check that they are not faulty

examiner's note Improving quality should lead to fewer mistakes, defects and returned goods. Some organisations try to get all employees involved in preventing defects. This is called total quality management.

 **89** **ANSWERS**

Lean production

Q1 State one benefit of lean production.

Q2 Lean production may involve producing with little or no stocks. This is called j........- i...- t........ production.

Q3 State one problem of holding low stock levels.

Q4 State three problems of introducing lean production.

ANSWERS

an approach to production that minimises the waste of resources such as time, people and money

A1 lower costs leading to higher profits; more efficient

A2 just-in-time

A3 may not be able to meet customer demands, leading to customer dissatisfaction; may not get bulk discounts when ordering supplies

A4 • finding the right suppliers
   • cost of training employees
   • cost of flexible equipment

***examiner's* note** Many firms have introduced lean production techniques to improve their efficiency and become more competitive. This requires very reliable suppliers.

ICT

Q1 Give examples of ICT that a business might use.

Q2 What is customer service?

Q3 How can having a website help customer service?

Q4 What is e-commerce?

ANSWERS

involves the use of information and communications technology: computing and communications systems

A1 website; e-mails; database; spreadsheets; word processing; design software

A2 business activities concerned with meeting customer needs as fully as possible (e.g. ensuring reliability, product information and good after-sales service)

A3 provides information and enables customers to order from anywhere in the world 24 hours a day; customers can keep track of their orders; can keep customers up to date with new products

A4 selling a product via the internet

examiner's **note** Developments in ICT can help businesses to communicate more effectively with their stakeholders, to gather and analyse data more effectively and to be more efficient.

 ANSWERS

External environment

Q1 State three economic factors that might affect a firm.

Q2 State two social factors that might affect a firm's success.

Q3 State three ways in which new technology may affect a business.

Q4 State three effects of an increase in competition.

ANSWERS

factors outside the control of a business that might determine its success

A1
- interest rates
- national income
- exchange rates
- inflation

A2
- population size
- average age of population
- social attitudes

A3
- new ways of producing
- new ways of marketing
- new products to produce
- increased efficiency

A4
- more choice for the customer
- lower prices
- greater incentive for innovation

examiner's **note** Successful firms plan ahead and try to anticipate change in the external environment.

Interest rates

Q1 What does the government spend its money on?

Q2 State two ways in which an increase in interest rates might affect a business.

Q3 How might a fall in consumer incomes affect a business?

Q4 State two ways in which an increase in unemployment might affect a business.

ANSWERS

A1 education; health; armed forces; police; benefits to people; grants to businesses

A2
- higher borrowing costs, which may reduce its borrowing and the borrowing of customers
- more expensive to repay loans

A3 may lead to less spending and a fall in sales

A4
- may lead to less demand as some customers will have lost their job and have less income
- may be easier to recruit

***examiner's* note** The interest rate is one of several economic factors that affect a business; others are consumers' income, employment levels and the price level.

Taxes

Q1 What is an indirect tax?

Q2 What is a direct tax?

Q3 What is the likely impact of higher taxes on demand?

Q4 State two reasons why a firm might not like government intervention.

ANSWERS

charges imposed by governments on individuals and firms

A1 a tax placed on goods or services, e.g. VAT

A2 a tax taken directly from earnings, e.g. income tax and corporation tax

A3 demand is likely to fall due to higher prices and/or less income after tax

A4 • may increase costs
   • may prevent it undertaking certain activities
   • more paperwork

***examiner's* note** The government spends money in many areas, such as education, welfare benefits, the police and defence. Taxation helps to raise revenue to pay for these services.

European Union (EU)

Q1 What is a tariff?

Q2 Is the UK a member of the EU?

Q3 State two benefits of being a member of the EU.

Q4 Many (but not all) countries within the EU have a single currency. What is it called?

ANSWERS

a group of European countries with free trade between them and a common external tariff

A1 a tax on foreign goods or services; this protects domestic firms

A2 yes

A3 • free trade (no tariffs and quotas)
   • free movement of people and money

A4 euro

***examiner's* note** Greater trade enables consumers to benefit from a wider range of goods than could be produced in their own country. It also provides firms with more markets for their goods.

Exchange rate

Q1 If £1= $1.6, what would a £300 UK good cost in the USA?

Q2 If £1= $1.6, what would a $32 US good cost in the UK?

Q3 What is a strong currency? Is a strong pound usually good for exporters? Explain your answer.

Q4 State two factors that would make UK firms more competitive internationally.

ANSWERS

the price of one currency in terms of another

A1 $480

A2 £20

A3 a currency that is expensive in terms of other currencies; it is not good for UK exporters because UK products would cost more money in foreign currency

A4 lower value of the UK currency making UK products cheaper abroad; greater innovation; greater efficiency and customer service; better marketing and design

***examiner's* note** There are many different exchange rates because there are many different currencies around the world and the pound has a price against each one. Changes in exchange rates affect firms that are exporting (because the price in foreign currency is affected) and importers (because the amount that has to be paid for foreign goods is affected).

 ANSWERS

Legislation

Q1 What is meant by the national minimum wage?

Q2 What is meant by competition policy?

Q3 Why does the government encourage competition?

Q4 State three elements of a contract of employment.

ANSWERS

government laws affecting individuals' and firms' behaviour

A1 determines the minimum amount someone must be paid in a job

A2 laws to ensure competition is fair (e.g. to prevent dominant firms exploiting consumers or price fixing)

A3 competition should lead to lower prices, innovation, greater efficiency, more choice for customers

A4 • terms and conditions of work and pay
  • holiday entitlement
  • notice period for dismissal
  • grievance procedure

***examiner's* note** The law can create opportunities for firms (e.g. opening up new markets) and protect them (e.g. as buyers), but it can also impose costs and restrict action.

 ANSWERS

Health and Safety at Work Act

Q1 The organisation responsible for implementing health and safety at work is the Health and Safety E...................

Q2 An organisation that protects employees' interests is called a t................. u..................

Q3 State three actions that may be taken if the Health and Safety at Work Act is not complied with.

Q4 State three benefits of a motivated workforce.

ANSWERS

legislation under which firms must
take reasonable steps to provide
a healthy and safe working environment

A1 Executive

A2 trade union

A3 • impose a fine
  • demand that the behaviour is changed
  • shut down the firm until it takes appropriate actions

A4 • better productivity
  • better attendance
  • greater willingness to cooperate

examiner's note Health and safety legislation protects employees at work;
other laws protect consumers and businesses.

Consumer protection legislation

Q1 State two laws that protect the consumer.

Q2 What other types of legislation can affect a firm?

Q3 What is the Data Protection Act?

Q4 What is meant by equal opportunities?

ANSWERS ▶▶

laws to prevent the consumer being misled or exploited

A1 • Sale of Goods Act
- Trade Descriptions Act
- Weights and Measures Act
- Supply of Goods and Services Act

A2 employment law, health and safety law, company law

A3 legislation to protect individuals who have information held about them on computer

A4 equal chances at work for all employees, regardless of gender, race, disability and sexual preference

***examiner's* note** Consumer laws may protect the buyer, but they impose costs and restrictions on the firms involved (e.g. labelling, the way products are made and restrictions on how they are promoted).

Environmental responsibilities of business

Q1 How can business activity affect the environment?

Q2 What is meant by sustainable business?

Q3 Why might behaving responsibly towards the environment help business?

Q4 How might the government encourage more environmentally friendly behaviour?

the obligations of business to protect the environment

A1 traffic congestion; air, noise and water pollution; global warming; the depletion of natural resources

A2 one that has no negative impact on the environment and does not deplete natural resources (i.e. uses renewable resources)

A3 attracts customers, employees and investors; saves money (e.g. by recycling and using less energy and resources)

A4 taxing undesirable behaviour or consumption (e.g. tax on petrol); legislation (e.g. on noise and pollution)

***examiner's* note** In recent years, many organisations have adopted more environmentally friendly policies due either to greater awareness of the issues or to a desire to be seen doing the right thing, or both.